ISBN 978-0-267-40052-2
PIBN 10727293

LOYAL CRUSADERS'
MANUAL.

CONTAINING

The Ritual, Rules, Regulations, and Plan of Work

OF THE

LOYAL CRUSADERS,

AN ORGANIZATION OF YOUNG PEOPLE, UNDER THE
CONTROL AND MANAGEMENT OF THE

Order of Sons of Temperance.

COMMITTEE:

REV. R. ALDER TEMPLE, M. W. P.,
F. M. BRADLEY, P. M. W. P.,
BENJ. R. JEWELL, P. M. W. P.,
BENJ. F. DENNISSON, P. M. W. P.,
EUGENE H. CLAPP, P. M. W. P.

PUBLISHED BY THE NATIONAL DIVISION
WASHINGTON, D. C.:
1890.

DEDICATORY.

—

TO

THE BOYS AND GIRLS OF NORTH AMERICA

THIS RITUAL GOES FORTH AS A

LOVING MESSAGE

FROM THE HEART OF ONE WHO PRAYS AND BELIEVES THAT

THROUGH THEIR EFFORTS AND INFLUENCE THIS CONTINENT

WILL BE DELIVERED FROM THE CURSE OF

STRONG DRINK.

THE AUTHOR.

SALUTATORY.

To the Sons of Temperance of North America, Greeting:

By order of the National Division, a new organization for children and youth has been called into existence. This 21st day of April, 1890, we present it to you and commend it to your love and fraternal watch-care. It is NEW in all respects, having a new, simple, and beautiful ritual, a new name, a new badge, new odes, and new supplies manufactured to order, for this special work by the National Division.

Ere we assemble in the City of New York in 1892, to celebrate the semi-centennial of our Order, we wish to have enrolled hundreds of thousands of

LOYAL CRUSADERS!

This is not extravagant. The children are ready, and you may organize them if you will. This continent is to be redeemed from the drink-curse by and through the education of the boys and girls of to-day. It is your privilege to participate in this educational work. We come to you, therefore, in full faith that you will aid to the extent of your ability in establishing and perpetuating the organization to be known as the

LOYAL CRUSADERS.

It is *your* work—do not shrink from it!

"With malice toward none, with charity for all, with firmness in the right as God gives us to see the right," we should solemnly and gladly take up this new duty and enjoy this new privilege. Our pledge of fidelity, taken at the altar of our beloved Order, binds us to never-ceasing warfare against drink. In the interests of the children let us renew this pledge, and maintain it as long as life shall last, and perhaps some of *us* and many of our Loyal Crusaders may live until this New World, redeemed from the thraldom of the liquor-crime, shall stand out in all its original loveliness, in God's pure sunshine, so that once again may be heard the blessed angel-song, coming down to us through the ages, "GLORY TO GOD IN THE HIGHEST, ON EARTH PEACE AND GOOD WILL TO MEN."

The Emblem of the Army of Loyal Crusaders is a shield bearing the device of a Water-lily and a Sword.

The Shield represents the Pledge of total abstinence, which is designed to protect the young from the evils of intemperance.

The Water-lily symbolizes purity of heart and life.

The Sword is a sign of warfare against strong drink and all evil habits, and also represents the law of Prohibition which is designed to destroy the manufacture and sale of all intoxicating drinks.

Motto :

LOVE, PURITY, AND FIDELITY.

Watchword :

IF GOD BE FOR US, WHO CAN BE AGAINST US?

War Cry :

DEATH TO ALCOHOL !

Colors :

RED, WHITE, AND BLUE.

INSTRUCTIONS

FOR ORGANIZING A COMPANY OF LOYAL CRUSADERS.

Every city, town and village in North America should have a Division of Sons of Temperance and a Company of Loyal Crusaders. From the Company the Division will constantly receive intelligent recruits, while Sons of Temperance engaging in children's work will have their own zeal quickened, their own pulses stirred, their own faith increased and strengthened.

On every hill-top and in every valley, where church bells invite the people to worship God, there are brave, true men, and tender, loyal women, whose hearts go out in love toward the children, and who delight in children's work. To such as these we wish to entrust the management of our army of Loyal Crusaders.

Our rules provide that the five *senior* officers shall be members of the Order of Sons of Temperance, except where this is clearly impossible, in which case the National Superintendent may authorize these positions to be filled by temperance workers who are not members of the Order, provided they shall first sign the pledge of the Sons of Temperance, and file it with the Superintendent. It is believed that in every such case the formation of a Division of "Sons" will follow at an early date.

The success and perpetuity of each company will depend on these five senior officers, especially the Worthy Commander. This officer, whether man or woman, should have the respect and confidence of the community, should be a lover of children, and should be adapted to the work. The other senior officers should likewise be of good report, men and women of character, to whose care and teaching fathers and mothers may willingly entrust their loved ones.

Our proposed army of Loyal Crusaders is not for little children *only*, but for all who are under fifteen years of age. Each company is divided into two sections, one of boys and the other of girls, and each section is again subdivided into three ranks, with a sergeant in charge of each rank. The age of each child determines its rank. (See form of organization.)

Wherever practicable, the company should be organized under the immediate patronage of a Division. Where this is impracticable, individuals are invited to correspond with the National Superintendent. Divisions and Grand Divisions are urged to proceed at once with this all-important work. Officers of Grand Divisions may render valuable assistance by furnishing to the National Superintendent the names of capable men and women interested in young people's work.

Each Division should promptly refer this matter to a committee of its most enthusiastic and faithful members, and this committee, after studying the rules, regulations, and instructions given in the Loyal Crusaders' Manual, should select a Worthy Commander, and report his or her name to the Division for approval. Then the committee should assist the Worthy Commander in choosing the other senior officers, and the senior officers should select from the children the *junior* officers. The name and post-office address of the Worthy Commander should be promptly reported to the National Superintendent, who may have special instructions for him or her.

Every Division has its musical members, and music is a power in children's organizations. Invite every singer and musical performer in the Division to help you in organizing and entertaining the young people In fact, give the entire Division something to do in this new movement.

Members of the old Order of Sons of Temperance, who believe that the permanent suppression of the drink traffic is to come through the education of the bright-eyed boys and sweet-faced girls of this North American continent, have now an opportunity to show their faith by their works! This army of Loyal Crusaders is YOURS. Every word of its beautiful ritual was written by a member of the Order. Every one of the odes comes from the pen of a member of the National Division. Its rules and regulations are all prepared in the interests of our beloved Order, and YOU are now invited to do your part of the work.

HOW TO INTEREST THE PEOPLE IN THE LOYAL CRUSADERS.

Arrange for a *successful* public meeting, in a church edifice, Sunday-school room, or public hall, as may be deemed best, but be sure to have a piano or organ to assist in the singing. Invite the pastors of the locality to attend, and also the Sunday-school superintendents and teachers, and all prominent citizens who believe in the welfare of the children and the perpetuity of good government. See that all these are *actually* invited. Then, through the Sunday-schools and public schools, summon the chil dren and young people. If they get the invitation, they will come. Printed cards, with the day, hour, and place, do not cost much, and will add materially to the size of your audience. Do not forget or neglect the parents of the children, for they must be always welcomed to both public and private meetings of the Loyal Crusaders. Ask the newspapers to give you a good notice of the meeting, and invite the editors and reporters to be present. Take a week, or two weeks if necessary, to prepare for this meeting, and make it a good one. Do not spoil it with long or dry speeches. Have lively singing. A recitation by one of the young people would be helpful.

Read briefly from the rules and regulations contained in the Manual, as to the object, pledge, motto, watchword, &c. Explain as to our beautiful badge which each recruit is to wear. Let them understand that the Captain, Lieutenant, Marshal, Herald, Guard, six Sergeants, two Bankers, and two Ensigns, are all to be selected from the boys and girls—that the company is to have a banner and a National flag, and that everything is to be bright and cheerful.

Then appoint a week-day—afternoon or night—to form a Company of Loyal Crusaders. Invite all children over five and under fifteen years of age to join. Circulate the application-cards. Where the children are small, be sure to gain the consent of parents, ere accepting them. Invite the parents to be present at the formation of the company, but no children except those who propose to " enlist."

Those in charge of the movement should carefully study the Manual so as to understand the sections, ranks, officers, &c. It is not expected that a Company of Loyal Crusaders will spring into perfection at its first meeting, as this is not possible, but you are invited to *go slow*, and *begin right*. This movement is not for a week, a month, or a year, but " for the war ! " Be prompt. Whatever is worth doing, should be well done.

Report the formation of the Company to the National Superintendent, on the blank form with which you will be furnished, and he will give you full instructions as to future movements.

Men and women are alike eligible to the five senior offices, and boys and girls are alike eligible to any of the junior offices.

The National Superintendent desires that every company shall be thoroughly equipped for service. This will require the expenditure of money. Your friends, if properly approached, will furnish many of the necessary supplies, and will donate money to purchase others. Do not be backward in asking for what you want. If *you* are willing to give your time and effort, the other friends of the children should contribute the funds. The Worthy Commander is therefore exhorted to see that his command is provided with everything necessary to make the organization attractive to the young people.

You will be furnished with two lists of supplies. The articles in one list will be supplied by the National Superintendent at the prices named. These are all manufactured to our order, of excellent materials, and furnished at actual cost. The supplies in the other list are to be furnished by each company.

It is the purpose of the National Division to make our Loyal Crusaders the brightest, happiest, and most aggressive children's organization in existence. Hand in hand our young people are to march across the Continent and rescue it from the grasp of our enemy Alcohol ! With banner and song, with sword and National flag, with the pledge as our shield, invoking the blessing and guidance of our Father in Heaven, our bright-faced army takes up its line of march !

Place no obstacles in the pathway of these dear ones, whose lives brighten so many homes, but give them your helping hand over the rough places in their onward and upward journey. You can not all be " worthy commanders," but you may cheer and encourage the young soldiers as they pass along. Their hearts are full of faith and hope and love. You can see this in the sparkling eye, the buoyant look, the quick step, the happy face. The world is all before them, and we may help them make their lives a psalm of praise to God, a benediction to the world ! They have enlisted for the war, and " The Retreat " is not found among their marching songs.

We who are older in years, yet young in spirit, will gain new strength for our own battles by looking into the hopeful faces of our Loyal Crusaders, who, overcoming all difficulties, building up pure, manly, and womanly lives, working out their salvation in the name of the crucified and risen Saviour, shall at last, one by one, reach the Beautiful City whose streets are of gold, whose walls are jasper, whose gates are pearl, and whose maker and builder is God !

INSTRUCTIONS TO WORTHY COMMANDERS.

1. The first and most important duty of a Worthy Commander is to see that the members of his Company are made comfortable and happy during their attendance at the meetings. The children should have only *pleasant* recollections of these meetings.

2. Before calling to order, the Worthy Commander should see that no children (under fifteen years of age) are present except members of his own or some other Company of Loyal Crusaders. Candidates should remain in an adjoining room until regularly enlisted.

3. The Marshal and Herald, under the supervision of the Worthy Commander, should see that the room is properly arranged for the meeting of the Company, as described in the diagram. They should also see that the books, cards, banners, &c., are in their proper places before the Company is called to order, and that they are carefully put away at the close of the meeting.

4. One rap of the gavel calls to order or seats the Company. Three raps call up the Company.

5. All officers should promptly take their stations when the Company is called to order. Vacancies should be filled as instructed in the opening exercises.

6. Every member is presented with the badge, either ribbon or silver, by the Company at the time of enlistment. This badge is to be the property of each member, and should be worn at every meeting, public or private. If lost or destroyed, the member should pay for a new one. The silver badges are beautiful, and should be kept for sale by the Company. They are furnished at actual cost by the National Superintendent.

7. The "Loyal Crusaders' Manuals" should be kept by the Worthy Commander, and should be loaned only to the officers to study their parts in the ceremonies. The enlistment exercises should be kept *private*, so as to have their full effect on the children when admitted to the company. No child, therefore, should be permitted to handle the Manual, who is not an enlisted member.

8. The Worthy Commander should carefully study the Manual and make himself thoroughly acquainted with the ritual, rules, regulations, and instructions that uniformity may be observed throughout our international jurisdiction. He should call the officers together, and rehearse with them the opening, enlistment, and closing ceremonies, and should urge all of them to become thoroughly familiar with the parts assigned them.

9. Keep the National Superintendent informed as to your progress; and write him for information and supplies whenever needed.

10. At public meetings see that every member wears the badge. Appoint a number of the larger boys to act as ushers, and the larger girls to take the collection. Give the children something to do.

11. Loyal Crusaders may remain in the company after they reach the age of fifteen, if they desire. The Worthy Commander should encourage every one to unite with a Division of Sons of Temperance when the age of fifteen is reached; thus giving them the protection of both organizations. This age is a critical period in life, especially with boys, who begin to realize that they are no longer children, but are old enough to take some part in the great world that lies before them.

12. Finally, brethren, whatsoever things are true, whatsoever things are honest, whatsoever things are just, whatsoever things are pure, whatsoever things are lovely, whatsoever things are of good report—*teach* them to the boys and girls confided to your care, that they may grow up into noble, honorable, useful manhood and womanhood.

SOLDIERS OF HONOR.

The pledge of the Loyal Crusaders is against liquor only. There are, however, other evils, intimately associated with the drink habit. From these we would protect our young people. We therefore have a "Soldiers of Honor Pledge" which is to be read at every Company meeting, and all who are perfectly willing to do so, may sign it. This pledge is not required as a test of membership, but is voluntary with each comrade.

SOLDIERS OF HONOR PLEDGE.

I solemnly pledge my honor that I will abstain from the use of tobacco in every form, and from all profane and vulgar language.

RECORD OF SOLDIERS OF HONOR.

The Secretary should keep a separate list of all who sign the "Soldiers of Honor Pledge."

DIAGRAM OF HALL.

Sec.

Capt.—W. C.—Lieut.

Treas.

1st Ser.
2d Ser.
3d Ser.

Banker

Boys' Section.

Table.

Girls' Section.

1st Ser.
2d Ser.
3d Ser.

Chap.

Banker.

Herald
Ensign.

Marshal.
Ensign.

Guard.

V. C.

ORDER OF BUSINESS.

1. Opening.

2. Calling Roll of Officers.

3. Enlistment Ceremonies.

(Recess.)

4. Receiving the Company offering.

W. C.—"The Bankers will now receive the Company offering." (The Bankers take the collection from their respective Sections, seat themselves at the table in the center of the room, count the amounts and make a note of the same. It is then turned over to the W. C., who announces which Section has contributed the largest sum. The Treasurer receives it, giving his receipt for it to the Worthy Commander.)

5. Promotion of Comrades.

W. C.—"Has any Comrade reached the age for promotion?" (Any Sergeant having transfers to make will report as follows:)

Sergeant.—"Worthy Commander, Comrade —— of —— Rank, having reached the age of ——, is respectfully reported for promotion."

(Three raps.)

W. C.—"The Marshal will present the Comrade."

"Comrade, may you grow in virtue and goodness, as well as in years, and continually strive to reach the highest rank in all that forms a true and noble character. You will now take your place in the rank which your age entitles you to enter."

(One rap.)

6. "Is any Comrade sick or in distress?"

7. Each Sergeant having privately reported to the Secretary the number present in his rank, the Secretary will here announce the total number present.

8. Program arranged by Entertainment Committee.

9. Closing.

RULES AND REGULATIONS.

NAME.

LOYAL CRUSADERS.

OBJECT.

To pledge young people to abstain from the use of intoxicating drinks; to instruct them concerning the nature and effects of alcoholic beverages, and narcotics; to teach them to regard the saloon and the liquor traffic as evils to be hated and destroyed.

MEMBERSHIP.

Boys and girls over five years of age and under fifteen years shall be eligible to membership.

PLEDGE.

I solemnly promise that I will not knowingly taste or touch any Wine, Beer, Cider, Brandy, Whisky, or any other drink that contains Alcohol.

MOTTO.—Love, Purity, Fidelity.

WATCHWORD.—If God be for us, who can be against us ?

WAR CRY.—Death to Alcohol.

COLORS.—Red, White, and Blue.

BADGE.

A Shield, bearing as a device, a sword and water-lily.

FORM OF ORGANIZATION.

The local branches shall be called companies and shall be designated alphabetically, beginning in each city, town, or village, with "Company A." In each company the boys shall constitute one section, and the girls another or separate section. Each section shall be divided into three ranks, and each rank shall be in charge of a sergeant. The first rank shall include those between the ages of twelve and fifteen years; the second rank shall include those between eight and twelve years, and the third rank all under eight years. The birth-day of each child shall be recorded, so that transfers may be made from the third to the second, and from the second to the first rank.

The companies (two or more) in any city, town, or village, shall constitute a battalion, to be numbered in each State or Province, according to the date of organization, and to take the name of the place where located, thus: "Washington Battalion No. 1," or "Victoria Battalion No. 1." Battalion commanders shall be appointed by the National Superintendent of Young People's Work.

OFFICERS.

The Senior Officers shall be as follows:

Worthy Commander, Worthy Vice-Commander, Chaplain, Secretary, Treasurer.

The Junior Officers shall be—

Captain, Lieutenant, Marshal, Herald, Guard.

Two Bankers—one boy and one girl.

Two Ensigns—one boy and one girl.

First, Second, and Third Sergeants—boys.

First, Second, and Third Sergeants—girls.

DUTIES OF OFFICERS.

The *Worthy Commander* shall have command of his Company, and shall preside at all meetings, private and public, unless on special occasions he prefer to invite some one to fill his place. He shall see that the rules and regulations of the Company are strictly observed, and that all other officers are prompt and efficient in the discharge of their duties. He shall see that the Company is fully supplied with temperance literature, books, cards, badges, and everything that is necessary to a perfect organization. He shall examine the semi-annual returns when prepared by the Secretary, for the Grand or National Division, and, if found correct, shall sign them, and have them forwarded to the proper officers. Under ordinary circumstances he shall be the judge of the fitness of applicants for admission to the Company, but if the correctness of his decision is doubted he shall summon the other Senior officers, and a majority shall decide.

The *Worthy Vice-Commander* shall take the part assigned him in the laws and ritual. In the illness or necessary absence of the Worthy Commander, he shall take command of the Company, and appoint some one to act as Worthy Vice-Commander.

The *Chaplain* shall open and close the meetings with prayer, and shall take the part assigned him by the laws, and in the ceremonies.

The *Secretary* shall keep a complete record of all the meetings and business of the Company. He shall record the date of admission and date of birth of each applicant. He shall also record the resignation or transfer of any member of the Company. He shall enter in his minutes the amount of money received at each regular or public meeting, and also any amounts contributed by friends, or realized from entertainments. The records should show the amounts expended, and for what purposes. The Secretary shall conduct the correspondence of the Company, and shall prepare the semi-annual returns for the Grand or National Division of Sons of Temperance. At the close of his term, he shall present to the Company a full report of the business of the term.

The *Treasurer* shall receive the funds at each meeting of the Company, and shall give a receipt therefor to the Worthy Commander. He shall pay all orders signed by the Secretary and the Worthy Commander, and at the end of his term shall present a full report of moneys received and expended. The Company should require a bond for the faithful performance of duty.

These five (Senior) officers shall be members in good standing in the Order of Sons of Temperance, unless this is clearly impossible, in which case the National Division Superintendent of Young People's Work may authorize these positions to be filled by temperance workers who are not members of the Order, provided they shall first sign the pledge of the Sons of Temperance, and file it with said Superintendent.

The Senior officers in charge of a Company at its organization shall fill their respective positions until the 31st of December following. In December of each year, these officers shall be chosen to serve one year. The Worthy Commander shall call a business meeting for this purpose, at such time as may be convenient, and shall notify all to be present who are entitled to vote. The voters shall be the Senior officers, the Junior officers, and all members of the first rank, and a majority of the votes shall elect.

(It is hoped that elections may generally be unanimous.) When the Company is under the immediate supervision of a Division, the names of the officers elected by the Company shall be submitted to the Division for approval. Should there be a disagreement between the Company and the Division relative to officers, the question shall be referred for decision to the National Superintendent. Vacancies may be filled at any time.

JUNIOR OFFICERS.

The Junior officers, at the organization, shall be selected by the Worthy Commander, and shall serve until the 30th of June, or 31st of December following, and thereafter these officers shall be elected in June and December of each year, by members of the first rank, on nomination of the Worthy Commander. Should any one nominated by the Worthy Commander be rejected, another nomination should be promptly made.

The Captain, Lieutenant, and other Junior officers shall take the parts assigned them in the opening, initiatory, and closing ceremonies, and they will be expected to memorize their respective parts.

The Sergeants shall be seated at the head of their respective ranks, and shall keep them in order, conduct them during the ceremonies, and at the close of each meeting collect the books and cards, and hand them to the Marshal or Herald. Each Sergeant shall keep a correct list of the members in his rank, with the age at entry, and shall transfer them to other ranks on reaching the required age, reporting his action to the Worthy Commander as instructed in the Ritual. Each Sergeant shall note carefully the names of absentees, and ascertain the cause of absence, and if any comrade shall be absent from two successive meetings, the Sergeant shall notify the Worthy Commander.

The Marshal and Herald shall be responsible for the property of the Company, shall see that it is properly arranged for the meetings, and that it is cared for at the close of each meeting.

The Ensigns shall have charge of the colors of the Company, the Bankers shall take the collection as specified in the order of business, and the Guard shall prevent unsuitable persons from entering.

COMMITTEES.

The Committees shall be as follows:

1st. *Committee on Entertainment,* to consist of the Worthy Commander, Worthy Vice-Commander, Captain, Lieutenant, and three comrades of the first rank, to be selected by the Worthy Commander. For each Company meeting, they shall provide entertaining and instructive exercises, either by adults or children, or both. Wherever practicable there should be a blackboard, and object lessons, and picture talks should be given. The children should be encouraged to take part in the exercises. This committee should also arrange for frequent public meetings.

2LCM

2d. *Finance Committee,* to consist of the Worthy Commander, Chaplain, and three comrades of the first rank to be appointed by the Worthy Commander. This committee shall devise plans for collecting money for the Company, and shall examine the books and vouchers of all officers and committees that handle the funds of the Company.

The Worthy Commander is authorized to appoint any other committees he may deem necessary.

RULES AND REGULATIONS.

1. The Company shall be supported by the voluntary contributions of its members and friends. Public entertainments should be occasionally given, with admission fee or collection. The Finance Committee should see that Sons of Temperance have an opportunity to contribute. The Division or Divisions in the locality should be invited to help pecuniarily and otherwise.

2. Every member of the Company shall wear the badge at all meetings, public and private, and *may* wear it at all other times.

3. At the regular meetings of the Company, those entitled to be present shall be as follows :

Members of the Company who have been duly admitted.

Members of other companies of "Loyal Crusaders."

Members of the Order of Sons of Temperance.

Parents or other adult relatives of members of the Company.

Ministers of the Gospel, Sunday-School Superintendents, and other temperance workers."

N. B.—Children under fifteen years of age, who are

not members of a Company of Loyal Crusaders, shall *not* be admitted to the regular meetings until proposed, accepted, and admitted as members.

4. The punishment for violation of pledge shall be at the discretion of the *Senior* officers of the Company. The most effective punishment for a child is forgiveness, kindness, and encouragement.

5. Members may be transferred from one company to another when desired. Transfer cards will be included in the list of supplies, and when a card is signed by the Worthy Commander and handed or mailed to the applicant therefor his membership shall cease.

6. Any member of the Company may resign membership at any time by notifying the Worthy Commander in writing, and any name may be dropped from the rolls by a vote of the Senior officers, for what they may deem sufficient cause.

7. It is recommended that meetings be held weekly, in day-time if practicable, and that meetings be not more than two hours in length. Different localities will, however, make such regulations on these points and others as will tend to the success of the organization.

8. Each Company shall have a banner bearing the same device as the badge, and shall also have a National flag. The banner and flag shall be in charge of the Ensigns, and shall be displayed at all meetings, public and private, of the Company.

9. It is recommended that two small, inexpensive banners be made or purchased, and used as prizes, the first to be placed at the head of the rank which intro-

duces the largest number of new recruits at the meeting, and the second one at the head of the section contributing the largest amount of money.

Also that each rank of boys and each rank of girls have a banneret, with the number of the rank, thus : "Boys, rank 1," or "Girls, rank 3."

10. Each Company shall make a semi-annual report to the Grand Division of Sons of Temperance within whose jurisdiction it is located, and an exact copy of each report shall also be mailed to the Superintendent of Young People's Work of the National Division. In jurisdictions where there is no Grand Division the report shall be made to the National Division. These returns shall be prepared and mailed during the first week of January and July of each year, on blanks prepared by the National Superintendent and furnished through Grand Scribes or otherwise.

11. The Worthy Commander and associate officers shall use all diligence to increase the numerical strength of the Company, and shall keep constantly in view the *object* of the army of Loyal Crusaders, which is : "To pledge young people to abstain from the use of intoxicating drinks; to instruct them concerning the nature and effects of alcoholic beverages and narcotics ; to teach them to regard the saloon and the liquor traffic as evils to be hated and destroyed."

OPENING SERVICE.

The Worthy Commander Presides.

[One rap calls the Company to order.]

Captain.—Attention! Company.

Herald.—The Worthy Commander is now ready to proceed with the opening exercises of Company —— of Loyal Crusaders of ————. Parents of the comrades of this Company, Sons of Temperance in good standing, and other adults eligible to admission under our rules are invited to remain. All under fifteen years of age who are not comrades in this or some other Company of Loyal Crusaders will please retire.

Worthy C.—The Marshal will see if the officers are at their stations and report.

Marshal.—Worthy Commander, the officers are all at their stations except—

[Names absentees.]

[The W. C. fills the vacancies, those in the Junior staff from the first rank, if practicable.]

Worthy C.—The Guard will allow no one to enter or retire during the opening, closing, or enlistment ceremonies.

[Three raps.]

[The W. C. and Captain give the military salute, which is returned by the Company.]

Worthy C.— Comrades : We have enlisted as a Company of Temperance soldiers, to be instructed and encouraged in our efforts to war against Strong Drink; to overcome all evil habits, especially the use of tobacco, and profane and vulgar language; and to be led in the paths of purity and truth.

Believing that no human efforts can be truly successful without Divine aid, we will now listen reverently while the Chaplain invokes God's blessing.

Chaplain.—Heavenly Father, we come to Thee for Thy help and Thy blessing. Inspire us with love for all that is pure and good. May we feel an earnest desire to be helpful to others, that we may win them from evil ways. Be Thou our Divine Commander in our battle with the hosts of sin, and grant us the victory at last, in the name of Jesus Christ, who has taught us to say—

[*Company repeats the Lord's Prayer in concert.*]

Worthy C.—We will sing our opening chorus.

Tune.—SPARKLING AND BRIGHT.—Page 41, " Ripples of Song."

> Happy and free as the birds are we,
>> And we bring a joyous greeting
> To comrades dear who are gathered here,
>> In our young Crusaders' meeting.
>
> As a temperance band we will bravely stand,
>> For help on God depending;
> For whenever we fight for the Truth and the Right,
>> His cause we are defending.

[*One rap.*]

Worthy C.—Comrades, what is the name of the enemy that we have pledged ourselves to fight against?

Company.—Alcohol.

Captain.—(*Rising.*) What is Alcohol?

Company.—The poisonous element that is found in all intoxicating drinks.

Captain.—Did God make Alcohol?

Company.—No.

Captain.—Where does it come from ?

Company.—From the decaying and fermenting of fruits and grain.

Captain.—What names does Alcohol take to deceive and ruin people ?

Company.—Beer, Wine, Cider, Brandy, Rum, Whiskey.

Captain.—Do all these drinks cause drunkenness ?

Company.—They do.

Captain.—What does the Bible say concerning intoxicating drinks ?

Chaplain.—Wine is a mocker and strong drink is raging, and whosoever is deceived thereby is not wise.

Worthy C.—There are other evil habits that deprave the morals and injure the health of the young. Name the two that ought to be condemned and shunned by all.

Company.—The use of tobacco and profane and wicked language.

Lieutenant.—Can our hearts be pure and our bodies healthy if we are slaves to these unclean and vicious habits ?

Company.—They can not.

Lieutenant.—What does the Bible say of those who are free from all evil and impure ways ?

Chaplain.—Blessed are the pure in heart, for they shall see God.

Lieutenant.—How can we live pure lives ?

Chaplain.—Only by God's help, which he will give us if we ask in the name of Jesus Christ, the Savior.

[*One rap.*]

Worthy C.—The Guard will now admit any who are entitled to enter.

ENLISTMENT CEREMONIES.

Worthy C.—Has any comrade the name of a volunteer to propose for enlistment in this Company?

Secretary.—(*Rising.*) Worthy Commander, Comrade —————— ——————— proposes (*Reads name, age, and residence.*) These volunteers have received the approval of the Worthy Commander.

Worthy C.—Comrades, all who are in favor of receiving these volunteers will raise the right hand. All opposed will manifest it by the same sign. I declare them elected. The Marshal will retire and see if there are any volunteers in waiting.

[*The Marshal retires and obtains the names of candidates.*]

Marshal.—(*Advancing to the center of the hall.*) Worthy Commander, I find the following volunteers waiting for enlistment. (*Reads names.*)

Worthy C.—The Marshal will retire and introduce them. (*The Marshal retires, arranges the volunteers in single file, and when ready notifies the Guard.*)

Guard.—Worthy Commander, the Marshal is ready to enter with the volunteers.

[*One rap.*]

Worthy C.—Comrades and visitors will maintain perfect order during the ceremony of enlistment. The Guard will admit them.

(*As the door is opened the Herald advances.*)

Herald.—Worthy Commander, the Marshal approaches with the volunteers. (*He returns to his station and* *when the candidates enter led by the Marshal, he takes his place at the end of the line and retains it during the ceremony.*)

[*Three raps.*]

[*Company sings:*]

Tune.—AULD LANG SYNE.

With hearts and voices we extend
A greeting of good cheer,
And gladly welcome to our ranks
Each temperance volunteer.

[*The candidates are slowly led around the room during the singing and placed before the Worthy Commander.*]

[*One rap.*]

Marshal.—Worthy Commander, I have the pleasure of introducing (*reads names*), who have been elected for enlistment in this Company.

Worthy C. (*Rising.*) MY DEAR YOUNG FRIENDS:—History tells us that Palestine, or the Holy Land where our Savior was born, was once captured by the Turks, who killed many of the Christians and treated others with the greatest cruelty.

At last, men banded together in great armies and marched against these wicked Turks. At one time thirty thousand boys joined them to aid in driving these tyrants from the Holy Land, and this is called in history the "Children's Crusade."

An enemy more fierce and cruel than the pagan Turk, has captured *our* native land. It slays thousands of people every year; it holds thousands in a terrible slavery, and it brings suffering, sadness, and sorrow into many hearts and homes.

We have joined in a crusade to protect ourselves and to rescue the captives of this wicked foe, who is known as *Alcohol,* the poisonous element that lurks in every kind of intoxicating drink, whatever may be its name. Its great power for evil lies in the fact that it comes in various forms to entice and entrap the young.

It sparkles in the glass of cider that many will tell you is harmless "apple juice."

It foams on the mug of beer that others will say is good for your health.

It gleams in the rosy-tinted wine that may be offered by the hand of a friend.

But, in whatever form it may come to tempt you, it is your enemy, and you must not be deceived by it.

Chaplain.—Who hath woe? Who hath sorrow?

Company.—They that tarry long at wine.

Chaplain.—Who hath contentions, and wounds without cause, and redness of eyes?

Company.—They that seek strong drink.

Chaplain.—Look not upon the wine when it is red; when it giveth its color in the cup.

Company.—At the last, it biteth like a serpent and stingeth like an adder.

Worthy C.—What is the best safeguard and shield against this deadly foe?

Company.—*The Pledge of Total Abstinence.*

Worthy C.—In olden times the soldier who went into battle carried before him a large metal plate called a shield, which protected him from the blows of the enemy.

The *Pledge* is our *shield.* As long as we hold to it and shelter ourselves behind it—looking up to God for help—

Alcohol can have no power over us. We must not forget it, or lay it aside for a single moment.

Our enemy often comes in a pleasing disguise, and is continually watching to find us unguarded. Beware !

[*Three raps.*]

You will now place your right hand on your heart and repeat after me the pledge.

PLEDGE.

I solemnly promise that I will not taste or touch any Wine, Beer, Cider, Brandy, Whiskey, or any other drink that contains Alcohol.

Chaplain.—May God bless you and keep you faithful to your promise.

Company.—Be faithful unto death !

[*Company sings.*]

Tune—AMERICA; OR, GOD SAVE THE QUEEN.

> Father, be near us now
> As we this solemn vow
>   Pledge Thee to-day.
> We know that we are weak,
> Strength from above we seek,
> Pure, faithful, brave, and meek,
>   Keep us, we pray.

Captain.—(*Advances and fastens badge on candidate's breast.*) I now adorn you with this badge, and proclaim you a Loyal Crusader. Never be guilty of any word or act that will bring disgrace upon it. Let the principles it represents shine in your conduct and beautify your life.

Lieutenant.—Comrade, we rejoice that another soldier has enlisted in the army that is battling against King Alcohol. We bid you welcome to the ranks of the Loyal Crusaders.

Company.—Welcome ! Comrade, welcome.

[*The candidates are placed before the Chaplain,*)

Chaplain.—(*Rising.*) In a grassy meadow, under the blue arch of the summer sky, there was a pond of water, with rushes and ferns fringing its edge, and sunbeams glancing like golden arrows over its quiet surface.

Away down at the bottom of this pond there was a tiny flower-bud all folded up in its dark-green covering.

As it looked up it could see the light of day dimly shining through the water, and soon it began to reach toward it. But there were snakes and worms and slimy, crawling creatures near it that clung about it and tried to hold it back. Some of them were as strong as they were hideous, and the little bud had to strive against them with all its might.

But it shook them off and went on climbing upward, and growing stronger as it came nearer to the light and sunshine.

At last it lay in its cradle of glossy, green leaves on the surface of the pond, a beautiful, snow-white lily, sending out from its golden heart a perfume so delicious that the birds sang more sweetly, the children laughed more gleefully as they passed, and all who saw it rejoiced in its beauty and fragrance.

Your soul is like the slowly unfolding lily-bud, and there are ugly creeping creatures, in the form of evil habits, that will try to fasten their grasp upon you and draw you away from purity and goodness. Pray always to God that you may be able to resist them, and with his help they will lose their power to harm you.

(*The following paragraph is to be omitted when the candidates are all girls.*)

Next to the use of intoxicating drinks, against which you have just been pledged, I must warn *you*, my *brother comrades*, that the use of Tobacco is a vice to be hated and shunned. It defiles the breath, degrades the morals, and injures the health. The cigarette is a deadly foe to health and purity.

The use of profane and vulgar language is another wicked habit, against which you must carefully guard your lips. You can not take the name of God in vain, nor utter wicked words, without dishonoring Him and losing your own self-respect.

(*The following paragraph to be omitted when the candidates are all boys.*)

You, my *sister comrades*, must always discourage and condemn in others the use of Tobacco, profanity, or other impure and degrading habits. Win them to a love for purer ways. You know not how strong your influence may be. Use it always for temperance and truth, and you will be happy in knowing that you are helping to make the world better.

The Water Lily is our emblem of Purity. May your young lives, like the snowy flower, grow upward in the sunshine of God's love, and blossom out into the fullness and fragrance of beauty and purity, that will shed their blessing on all around you.

Company.—Keep thyself pure !

[*Three raps.*]

[*Company sings.*]

Tune.—I AM SO GLAD THAT JESUS LOVES ME.
(Music in Gospel Hymns, Consolidated or No. 1.)
Pure as the lily so fragrant and fair,
Seeking the sunlight of God's loving care;

Upward and onward our pathway must lead,
Shunning all evil in thought, word, and deed.
Striving with gentle pleading to win
Souls from the ways of error and sin;
Ever while gathering straying ones in,
Keeping our own hearts pure.

[The candidates are led around the room and placed before the Vice-Commander.]

[One rap.]

Vice-Com.—(*Rising*). When the crusaders of olden times went to war, they used their swords to kill their enemies. We use the sword also; not for the shedding of blood, but as a sign of warfare against Strong Drink, and an emblem of the law which is to destroy its great stronghold and headquarters—the Saloon.

Comrades, what is a Saloon?

Company.—A place where alcoholic drinks are sold, and where drunkards are made.

Vice-Com.—Is it a good or an evil place?

Company.—It is evil always and everywhere.

Vice-Com.—How do we know that it is?

Company.—A tree is known by its fruits.

Vice-Com.—What are the fruits of the Saloon?

Company.—Drunkenness, vice, poverty, crime, disease, murder, death.

Vice-Com.—Men get the privilege of carrying on the business that causes these evils by paying a sum of money, called a license fee; but there are many places, both in the United States and in the Dominion of Canada, where men can not buy a license to make drunkards. What prevents them?

Company.—The law of *Prohibition*.

Vice-Com.—What is the law of Prohibition?

Company.—A law that forbids the selling of intoxicating drinks.

Vice-Com.—Why do the saloon-keepers and beer brewers and their friends spend so much time and money in fighting the Prohibition law?

Company.—Because it breaks up their business.

Vice-Com.—(*To candidate.*) Comrade, we all agree that a business which causes so much wickedness, poverty, and suffering *ought* to be broken up, and it is the duty of every Loyal Crusader to help in this work. You can plead with people to vote for the destruction of the saloon, as *you* mean to do when you are old enough. You can sing for it and talk for it, and get others to thinking about the subject, for we depend on our young temperance soldiers to do grand work for our cause.

Comrades, what does the Sword on our banner and badge represent?

Company.—The sword is a sign of warfare against strong drink and all evil habits, and also represents the law of Prohibition, which is designed to destroy the manufacture and sale of intoxicating drinks.

Vice-Com.—When you are old enough to vote what will you do with the Prohibition sword?

Company.—Use it with brave and steady hand,
　　　To drive the Rum King from the land.

[*Three raps.*]

[*The candidates are faced about and placed in front of the table. The Ensigns advance with their colors and stand with their backs to the desks of the Secretary*

*and Treasurer, and about three feet distant from them.
Captain and Lieutenant take their places in front of the
Ensigns.]*

Captain.—Forward, March !

*[The instant the command is given to "March," the
Sergeants of the third ranks lead their soldiers out and
fall into line behind the Ensigns.   The second and first
follow in order, and they march down to the end of the
room, then turn and march up.   The Worthy Commander
advances to the table and the two lines meet behind him,
forming a semi-circle three ranks deep, the Sergeants of
the two sections meeting in the center.   The Captain
and Lieutenant take their places on either side of the
Worthy Commander.]*

[Company sings while marching.]

Tune.—MARCHING THROUGH GEORGIA.

Raise our banner, comrades, march ! with earnest hearts and true,
Close beside it, carry high, the old Red, White, and Blue;
Pledged to Total Abstinence, we love our Country, too,
    While we are marching to victory.

CHORUS.—Hurrah ! hurrah ! we'll bring the jubilee,
    Hurrah ! hurrah ! our Nation will be free;
    Shout for Prohibition till it rings from sea to sea,
    While we are marching to victory.

2.

How the drunkard's children will rejoice to see the day,
When their father's tempter shall be driven far away !
Death to Alcohol ! the battle cry we sound to-day,
    While we are marching to victory.

CHORUS.—Hurrah ! etc.

Worthy C.—Comrade, the true soldier is always cour-
ageous. Say *no*, boldly and bravely, whenever you are

tempted to violate your solemn promise, or to do anything you know to be wrong.

Be gentle and courteous to all, especially to your younger comrades. They will look to your example; let it be worthy of imitation.

Obey all the rules of the Company as laid down in the Loyal Crusader's Manual.

When you address the Worthy Commander salute him thus (*raising the right hand to the forehead.*)

Never leave the room while the Company is in session without rising and asking to be excused ; and always, on entering or leaving, salute the Vice-Commander, whose station is at the other end of the room.

Get volunteers for your Company whenever you can. Every one that is added to our ranks, weakens the enemy and hastens our victory.

Always speak kindly to the poor drunkard, and plead with him to sign the pledge and be a better man.

Be very gentle and pitiful to the drunkard's children. There are many sad-hearted little ones who suffer from cold, hunger, and cruelty, because of Strong Drink. They need all the help and sympathy you can give them.

Above all, remember that God sees you, and expects you to do your duty as a brave, true, temperance soldier, who is not afraid to stand up for the right, however strong the enemy may be.

Company.—If God be for us, who can be against us ?

Captain.—Next to the air we breathe, God's best gift to us is water. Men kill and spoil the delicious fruit and

3LCM

wholesome grain, and bring forth from their decay and
death, the Spirit of Evil we call Alcohol, which burns
and poisons and ruins the bodies and souls of its
victims.

Lieutenant.—(*Holding up glass.*) God's bright bever-
age cools, purifies, and blesses all his creatures.

Comrades, which do we choose, Alcohol or Water ?

Company.—Water, pure and clear and free.

God's own gift to you and me.

[*The Captain fills a glass for himself and one for each
candidate. The Marshal passes them.*]

Captain.—In this precious, life-giving drink, we
solemnly pledge ourselves to be true to our vows, true
to each other and true to God.

Chaplain.—The faithful shall drink of the water of
life.

[*They drink and the glasses are replaced on the table
by the Marshal.*]

Worthy C.—(*Shaking hands.*) Comrade, we welcome
you most cordially. May the lessons you receive here
be a great blessing to you, and may you prove in all
your words and deeds a fearless and worthy Loyal
Crusader. You will hereafter receive your enlistment
certificate.

Captain.—Comrades, salute your newly enlisted comrade.

[*The military salute is given promptly.*]

Captain.—Forward, March !

[*The Company marches down to the end of the room as
before, Captain and Lieutenant leading. The Ensigns
leave the ranks on reaching their stations, and the ranks
file into their places in order.*]

[*Company sings while marching.*]

Tune—RED, WHITE, AND BLUE.

(Music on page 72 of "Ripples of Song.")

An army of Loyal Crusaders,
 We rally for Temperance and Truth;
We bring to this contest with Evil
 The hope and the courage of youth.
We know there are hearts full of sorrow,
 And homes that are robbed of all joy;
And so we have banded together,
 Humanity's foe to destroy.

CHORUS.—With courage to dare and to do,
  For a cause that is noble and true,
  We'll stand by our colors like heroes,
  Three cheers for the Red, White, and Blue.

Worthy C.—The Marshal will now introduce you to the Sergeant whose rank your age entitles you to enter.

[*The Worthy Commander, Captain, and Lieutenant resume their stations.*]

Worthy C.—I now declare a recess till the sound of the gavel.

[*One rap.*]

CLOSING.

[*Three raps.*]

Captain.—Attention, Company!

Worthy C.—Comrades, the hour has arrived for us to break ranks and return to our homes.

May the instruction and the pleasure we have received leave their influence on our hearts and encourage us in our efforts to be good and to do good.

What does our motto, Love, Purity, and Fidelity, require us to do?

Company.—To love God, to keep our hearts pure, and to be faithful to our pledge.

Worthy C.—As many temptations may beset us before we meet again, we will solemnly renew our pledge, and carry it with us as our safeguard and Shield.

Every comrade will place the right hand on the heart and repeat after me.

THE PLEDGE.

CLOSING SONG.

" Thy love is better than wine."
(Page 16 " Ripples of Song.")

Worthy C.—We will now listen to the Chaplain.

Chaplain.—Our Father in Heaven, we pray that Thou wilt protect these young temperance soldiers from evil and enable them to withstand all temptation.

Fill their hearts with love to Thee and keep them faithful to their vows. And when the battle of life is ended and the last roll-call is heard, may each one answer joyfully, "Lord, here am I."

We ask it in the name of Jesus Christ our Savior. Amen.

INSTALLATION OF OFFICERS.

W. C.—The Secretary will read the names of the officers-elect.

Sec.—Worthy Commander, the following-named comrades have been elected as Junior Officers of this Company for the ensuing term. (*Reads names.*)

W. C.—The Vice-Commander, assisted by the Marshal, will receive from the retiring officers their books, cards, etc., and arrange them in order on the table in front of the W. C. The Vice-Commander will now present to me the officers-elect for installation.

(*The V. C. places the officers-elect in order before the W. C.*)

W. C.—(*Three raps*). Comrades, you have been elected by this Company of Loyal Crusaders to fill honorable and responsible positions. You will now be instructed as to your duties.

The *Guard* will have charge of the door; will prevent unsuitable persons from entering, and will preserve order in the ante-room.

The *Herald* will perform the duties assigned in the ritual, and will assist the Marshal in caring for the property of the Company.

The *Marshal* will perform the duties assigned in the ritual, and, assisted by the Herald, will see that the books, cards, colors, and other property of the Company are in readiness for the opening; and carefully returned to their places at the close.

The *Bankers* will take the Company offering or collection from their respective sections. They will count the amounts at the table in front of the W. C., who announces which section has contributed the largest sum.

The *Sergeants* will take charge of their respective ranks and will perform the duties required by the ritual. They will keep a complete list of their comrades, reporting the name and age of those who are entitled to promotion; also the names of those becoming Soldiers of Honor.

The *Ensigns* will have charge of the flag and banner; they will carry them during the enlistment exercises and at all public meetings and parades.

The *Lieutenant* will perform the duties required by the ritual, and will assist the Captain in taking charge of the Company.

The *Captain* will have command of the Company, subject to the authority of the Worthy Commander; will perform the duties required by the ritual, and in every way strive to be a brave, courteous, and faithful leader.

Each officer will place the right hand on the heart. Comrades, do you each one promise to become familiar with the duties of your office, and strive to perform them to the best of your ability? If so, please answer, "I do." You will now receive your books, cards, colors, and official emblems. (The V. C. presents them.)

May you ever prove worthy of the honors which your comrades have bestowed upon you. The Vice-Commander will now escort you to your stations.

(*Tune*—AULD LANG SYNE.)
With honor may we ever fill
Each station we may hold,
Our duties faithfully perform—
For truth be firm and bold.

May love inspire every heart,
And purity combine
With strong fidelity, to make
Our lives with beauty shine.

CPSIA information can be obtained
at www.ICGtesting.com
Printed in the USA
BVHW04*0739150818
524470BV00016B/53/P